Wonder Kitty Says It's Best to Pay Attention

Author: Howard Binkow
Illustrator: Max Alnutt

"Hi, I'm Wonder Kitty. Paying attention means to know what's happening around us. It helps us make better choices. Check it out."

While Luke Lion was looking at and licking a lime popsicle, he kicked the ball into his team's goal by mistake. He was in BIG trouble.

Wonder Kitty said, "Luke, it's best to know what's happening."

Later in the game, Luke knew what was happening and kicked the ball towards the other team's goal. He made a better choice.

Charley Horse hit a tree while playing video games on his bike. He was in BIG trouble.

Wonder Kitty said, "Charley, it's best to know what's happening."

After Charley's bike was fixed, he knew what was happening, missed the tree, and stayed safe. He made a better choice.

Wally Walrus was watching cartoons and got on the wrong school bus. He was in BIG trouble.

Wonder Kitty said, "Wally, it's best to know what's happening."

The next day, Wally put his iPad away. He knew what was happening and got home safely. He made a better choice.

Mooshie Moosie was busy picking his nose. He didn't notice his pants were falling down and that he forgot to tie up the family boat. He was in BIG trouble.

Wonder Kitty said, "Mooshie, it's best to know what's happening."

Someone nice brought the boat back. This time, Mooshie knew what was happening and tied up the boat. He made a better choice.

Funky Elephant was busy thinking about what he wanted for his birthday and forgot to tie down his tent. He was in BIG trouble.

Wonder Kitty said, "Funky, it's best to know what's happening."

In a few minutes, Funky saw what was happening and tied down the tent. He made a better choice.

Rocky Rhino put his school money under his hat instead of into his pocket as he was told to do. When he tried to pass gas and burp at the same time, his hat blew off and so did the money. He was in BIG trouble.

Wonder Kitty said, "Rocky, it's best to know what's happening."

The next day, Rocky knew what was happening and put the money deep in his pocket.
He made a better choice.

Zeekie Zebra took a nap in class and dreamed school was over. While he was sleeping, school was over and he missed the bus He was in BIG trouble.

Wonder Kitty said, "Zeekie, it's best to know what's happening."

The next day, Zeekie stayed awake in class. He knew what was happening so he could learn more and be the best he could be. He made a better choice.

While Punky Monkey was daydreaming about being an only child, the baseball went through his legs and his team lost. He was in BIG trouble.

Wonder Kitty said, "Punky, it's best to know what's happening."

The next game, Punky knew what was happening. He threw the batter out and his team won. He made a better choice.

Lucky Leopard threw his phone in the water for his dog to bring back instead of throwing a stick. He was in BIG trouble.

Wonder Kitty said, "Lucky, it's best to know what's happening."

Lucky borrowed his sister's phone. This time, he knew what was happening and carefully put the phone on a table. He made a better choice.

Wonder Kitty Says It's Best to Pay Attention
Wonder Kitty Says We Can All See God

Author Howard Binkow
Illustrator: Max Alnutt
Book Design: Jane Darroch Riley

We Do Listen Non-Profit Foundation
Home of the Howard B. Wigglebottom Series
www.wedolisten.org

First printing September 2017

ISBN: 978-0-9910777-8-6
LCCN 2017913379

Copyright ©2017 Howard Binkow Living Trust. No part of this book may be reproduced, stored in retrieval systems or transmitted in any form, by any means, including mechanical, electronic, photocopying, recording or otherwise without the prior written permission from the Trust.

Made in United States
Orlando, FL
09 November 2022